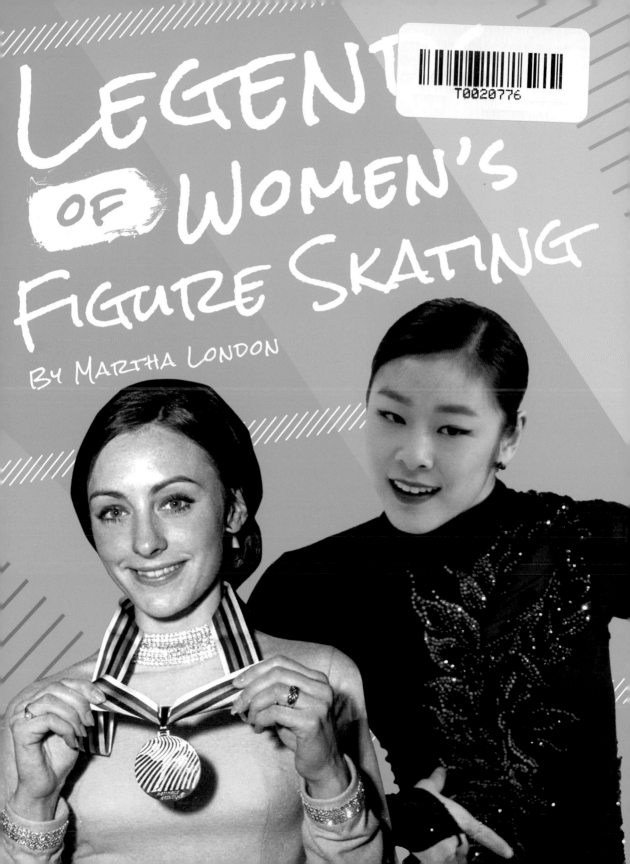

LEGENDS OF WOMEN'S FIGURE SKATING

BY MARTHA LONDON

Book design by Sarah Taplin
Cover design by Sarah Taplin

Photographs ©: AP Images, cover (left), 1 (left), 6, 12, 14; Ivan Sekretarev/AP Images, cover (right), 1 (right); Paul Chiasson/The Canadian Press/AP Images, 4; RDB/ullstein bild/Getty Images, 9; Bettmann/Getty Images, 10; stf/AP Images, 17; AP Images, 18; NewsBase/AP Images, 21; Eric Draper/AP Images, 22; Robert Skinner/The Canadian Press/AP Images, 24; Darron Cummings/AP Images, 27; Lynn Hey/AP Images, 28

Press Box Books, an imprint of Press Room Editions.

ISBN
978-1-63494-282-9 (library bound)
978-1-63494-300-0 (paperback)
978-1-63494-336-9 (epub)
978-1-63494-318-5 (hosted ebook)

Library of Congress Control Number: 2020913881

Distributed by North Star Editions, Inc.
2297 Waters Drive
Mendota Heights, MN 55120
www.northstareditions.com

Printed in the United States of America
012021

About the Author

Martha London works full-time writing children's books.
When she isn't writing, you can find her hiking in the woods.

TABLE OF CONTENTS

CHAPTER 1

BEGINNINGS

Alina Zagitova skated to center ice at the 2018 Olympics. The Russian skater was only 15 years old. But she was ready to show what the next generation of Russian skaters had in store for the world.

Zagitova's movements matched her upbeat music as she hopped and twirled across the ice. Then the music changed. It was slower. Zagitova began a series of jumps. As her toe pick dug into the ice, she gracefully leapt into the air. She tucked her arms in and spun. She landed

Alina Zagitova displayed balletic grace while sewing up the Olympic gold medal.

seven triple jumps. For triple jumps, skaters spin three times in the air. Big jumps like triples are harder to land at the end of a routine when skaters are tired. But Zagitova showed she had plenty of energy. Her difficult routine earned her an Olympic gold medal.

Many legendary skaters paved the way for Zagitova. One of the first big stars was Sonja Henie. She competed for Norway in the 1924 Olympics when she was only 11 years old. Henie placed last. But she did not give up. She attended the next three

Sonja Henie trains in Germany before the 1936 Winter Olympics.

Olympics and won gold at each. Henie is the only skater to win three gold medals in women's singles. And only one other skater has won gold twice.

In many ways, Henie changed the sport. Her free skate at the 1932 Olympics was different from any other before her. Henie was so graceful, some said she appeared to be floating as she landed her jumps. She later skated in touring exhibitions. She also starred in movies. But her Olympic success helped make figure skating widely popular.

Henie inspired women around the world. Tenley Albright and Carol Heiss were two of the first great American skaters. Albright began skating when she was eight years old. But then

Tenley Albright took silver in 1952 before winning gold four years later.

she became sick with polio. She lost a lot of strength. After she recovered, Albright began skating again. She won the 1956 Olympic gold medal. That made her the first American woman to do so in figure skating. Albright did not perform difficult jumps. Instead, her graceful style won over judges and fans.

Albright edged out Heiss at the 1956 Olympics. But Heiss beat Albright at the World Championships that year. The title was passed on. Heiss won a gold medal at the 1960 Olympics. She was the first woman to land the difficult double axel in competition.

Carol Heiss won five straight World Championships in women's singles.

CHAPTER 2

GROWTH

Throughout the 1950s, the United States dominated world figure skating. But tragedy struck in 1961. The US figure skating team was flying to the World Championships in Belgium. But the plane crashed. Every member of the team was killed. It took years for US figure skating to recover.

Peggy Fleming was just 12 years old at the time. Her coach died in the crash. But she would represent the rebirth of the US team. Elegant and stylish, Fleming won

Peggy Fleming helped lift US women's figure skating from tragedy to triumph in 1968.

Dorothy Hamill waves to the crowd after receiving her gold medal at the 1976 Winter Games.

five US titles and three World Championships in the 1960s. Her career highlight was winning gold at the 1968 Winter Olympics. It was the first US gold medal since the crash. It was also the only gold medal for any US athlete at the 1968 Games.

Fleming passed the baton to another young skater who captivated the nation. As a teenager, Dorothy Hamill practiced seven hours each day. It paid off with a gold medal at the 1976 Winter Olympics. Hamill was known for her short hair and a unique spin. The "Hamill camel" went from a camel spin to a sitting spin. A camel spin has one leg straight out. This spin became Hamill's trademark.

Women continued to push the envelope. Spins and jumps became more important as routines became more complex and difficult. For example, Hamill was the last skater to

DEBI THOMAS
California native Debi Thomas went to the Olympics in 1988. She impressed judges with her grace on the ice. She won a bronze medal. That made her the first Black athlete to medal in the Winter Games. She continued her studies at Stanford University while she was training for the Olympics.

win Olympic gold without performing a triple jump. The next generation of skaters were encouraged to showcase their athletic abilities in addition to their grace and technical skills.

Katarina Witt was one of the athletic skaters who signaled the sport's future. Witt was from East Germany. Her most memorable skates came in the Olympics.

In the 1984 Winter Games in Sarajevo, Yugoslavia, Witt edged out American Rosalynn Sumners for gold. She repeated her gold-medal performance four years later in Calgary, Canada. In doing so, she joined Sonja Henie in an exclusive club. They are the only two skaters to win back-to-back gold medals in women's singles.

Katarina Witt skates her final performance in Calgary. It earned her a second straight gold medal.

CHAPTER 3

GOLDEN ERA

Kristi Yamaguchi began skating when she was six years old. At first, it was a form of physical therapy. She was born with a foot abnormality. Skating helped Yamaguchi strengthen her leg muscles. But soon, it was clear she had a passion for skating. Yamaguchi was inspired by Dorothy Hamill. She watched Hamill's 1976 Olympic performance on TV. Yamaguchi even owned a Dorothy Hamill doll.

At first, Yamaguchi competed in mixed pairs. But in 1991, she switched

Kristi Yamaguchi was relatively new to singles competition when she won Olympic gold in 1992.

to singles. She qualified for the 1992 Winter Olympics. Yamaguchi was nervous before her performance. But then she was surprised by a visit from her idol, Hamill. She advised Yamaguchi to relax, do her best, and have fun.

Yamaguchi competed against Japanese star Midori Ito at the Olympics. Ito was famous for being the first woman to land a triple axel. A triple axel is a jump that includes three spins in the air. The skater takes off facing forward and lands facing the opposite way. The extra half turn makes the triple axel one of the most difficult jumps. Ito landed a triple axel at the 1992 Olympics. But it wasn't enough to win. Yamaguchi took home the gold.

Yamaguchi's US teammate Nancy Kerrigan took bronze that year. But Kerrigan was not satisfied. She continued to work, dreaming

Nancy Kerrigan won two medals in two Olympic appearances.

of a gold medal. Despite an injury at the 1994 Olympic trials, she made the team. Her style and grace made her a crowd favorite. Many expected her to win gold. However, she was upset by Ukrainian teenager Oksana Baiul.

Michelle Kwan was an alternate for the US team at the 1994 Olympics when she

was only 13 years old. She would go on to become one of the best skaters of her generation.

Kwan had many talents. She could outjump less athletic skaters. But she was more than a great jumper. Her style was expressive. Kwan's graceful skating matched the emotions in the music.

Despite her skill, Kwan never won Olympic gold. She took silver in 1998 and bronze in 2002. However, she won five world titles and inspired many young women to follow her path.

Michelle Kwan is one of the most decorated skaters of all time.

CHAPTER 4

MODERN STARS

Yuna Kim was far from home. The powerhouse skater from South Korea began training in Canada in 2006. Away from the South Korean media, Kim could concentrate. Yuna Kim was a household name in her home country.

She captured people's attention with her complicated yet graceful routines. Kim competed at the 2010 Olympic games. Her routine included seven triple jumps. It earned her high marks. She took home the gold medal.

In addition to her Olympic gold medal, Yuna Kim won two World Championships.

At the 2014 Olympics, Kim was favored to repeat her win. But a new Russian skater appeared on the ice. Adelina Sotnikova seemed untested. She had not won any World Championship medals prior to her Olympic debut. But her performance surprised everyone. She beat Kim to win the gold medal.

Figure skaters continue to push the boundaries of what is possible. The first woman to land a double axel was Carol Heiss in 1953. It took 35 years before Midori Ito landed a triple axel in 1988. Most people assumed women could not complete a quadruple jump. Quads require immense strength and leaping ability. However, female figure skaters didn't let anyone tell them what was possible.

In a quad jump, a skater turns four times in the air. In 2002, Miki Ando of Japan became the

Adelina Sotnikova seemingly came out of nowhere to shock the world in 2014.

first woman to land a quad in competition. Only a few women since Ando have been able to land a quad. However, more and more skaters began to practice this challenging jump.

Alysa Liu won the US national title in women's singles in 2019 and 2020.

One reason for this change is that several top-level Russian skaters began to master the quad. As the jump become more common, more skaters felt pressure to master the skill.

In 2019, Alysa Liu became the first American to land a quad jump in competition. She probably would have been a lock to make the US Olympic team. But Liu was still too young. In 2020, she was only 15 years old. Due to recent rule changes, she could not compete at the international level yet. Still, Liu had shown enough skill and talent that legends including Michelle Kwan predicted big things for her going forward.

There is no doubt female skaters continue to redefine the sport. What once seemed impossible is now expected. Athletes continue to raise the bar.

RUSSIAN STARS

Evgenia Medvedeva is an incredible Russian skater. She wowed judges with her technical and artistic skills on the ice. In 2017, she became the first woman in 16 years to win back-to-back World Championships. She was expected to take gold at the Olympics, too. But she lost to her teammate Alina Zagitova at the 2018 Olympics.

MILESTONES

1936

Sonja Henie wins her third straight Olympic gold medal.

1968

After an eight-year drought, Peggy Fleming wins a gold medal for the United States.

1988

Midori Ito becomes the first woman to land a triple jump in competition.

2002

Miki Ando is the first woman to land a quadruple jump in competition.

2014

Adelina Sotnikova becomes the first Russian woman to win an Olympic gold medal in singles figure skating.

2018

Alina Zagitova and Evgenia Medvedeva lead Russia to a gold and silver finish at the 2018 Winter Olympics.

GLOSSARY

alternate
An athlete who is available to compete if a teammate is unable to.

axel
A jump in figure skating from the outer forward edge of one skate with 1.5 turns taken in the air and landing on the outer back edge of the other skate.

debut
First appearance.

pairs
A type of competition in which two skaters perform as a team.

physical therapy
Treatment to help strengthen muscles after an illness or injury.

polio
An illness that causes flu-like symptoms and can cause permanent damage to the arms and legs.

routine
A series of movements in a performance.

TO LEARN MORE

To learn more about legendary women's figure skaters, go to **pressboxbooks.com/AllAccess**. These links are routinely monitored and updated to provide the most current information available.

INDEX